withdrawal

bland

ISBN: 9798364529930

CONTENTS

The Pleasure Demon

i roast my brain

over an open flame

until the room

smells like gasoline

after passing

through smoke,

the pleasure demon

greets me

"eat up, child

lie down"

its voice

is so warm

like a hug

and i had

been so weary,

so tired

it pulls a blanket
over my shoulders
and turns on
the television

"nothing too difficult
please" i croak
"of course not,
my child"

color and resolvable
conflict dance across
the beaten screen,
i've seen this one:

the lonely child, afraid
of their idiosyncrasies,
alienates themselves

their disappearance
is hardly noticed, but
by a select few

who search far and wide

across plains and mountains

until he is found

upon his return

the village celebrates

and he finally feels

accepted

"why can't life be

like this?" i ask

but the demon

is already gone

Portrait of a Silhouette

- lung full of black holes,

gasoline fuels the engine;

keep running away

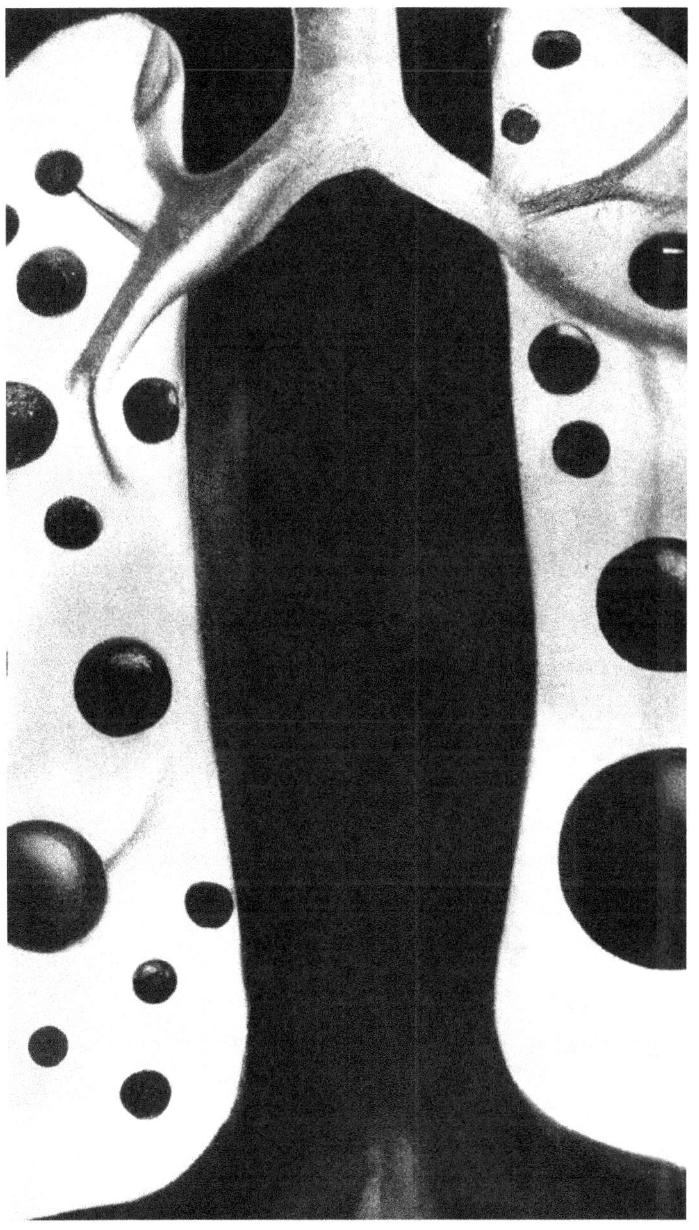

Fashioned

into an uncomfortable numbness,
the ever-present lantern glows and
fights the dead, lonely absence of all
things on the coldest of wintery nights

soft-spoken words are rehashed
and rehearsed to fit the narrative
of a wild beast, who drags bodies
in poorly wrapped cigarettes

unnoticed and undressed by the
pantomime. "but who cares?"
is valid only as an afterthought
and quickly forgotten as oil

seeps through the gaps between
our hands and disappears in the arid
soil below unaffordable designer shoes.
there are snakes somewhere

in the grass nearby

which will surely

bite at our heels

but at least they're Gucci.

Garbage Time

a glass of orange juice

and two pieces of fried chicken

fifteen minutes before midnight

to kill the taste

of weed on my

breath

in five minutes

i'll cough black mucus

into a toilet bowl

in twenty

i'll lie in bed

wondering where

the time went

then i'll turn

to my phone,

and waste thirty

minutes to an hour

reading the

thoughts of others,

and arbitrating

their memories,

most of which

i will forget

by sunrise

How Time Affects Memory

footprints in the dusty

aged linoleum

and scratchy sweaters

with frayed sleeves

hung forever

there's an imprint

on the wall, a scorch

mark that looks like

the outline of

an angel

or a wilting

flower, or a

car crash

you're home

the entryway is

a mess of

of memories

and light

and fire

a cacophony

of constant mutterings

lies beneath the surface

and

the walls

stretch thin

behind

pictures you

recognize only

faintly

there's still

shit in the litter box,

and coffee grounds

in the french press

but you smell

only the

dying

flowers

but you smell

only the

dying

flowers

carve into your wood

house become
toy soldier
and carry
everything but
your soul

burn bright
like a witch
and pay
for sins
you didn't mean
to get attached to

then collapse
a tired cluster
of resources
held together
by nothing
but dusty
memories

and fool's

gold

leaving feels

like coming,

only worse

the home,

no longer

a home

hangs in

the air like

a dying star

insects die

into the ground

endlessly

the same way

they will next

time

footprints ~~in the dusty~~

~~aged linoleum~~

and scratchy sweaters

~~with frayed sleeves~~

~~hung forever~~

~~there's~~ an imprint

on the wall~~, a scorch~~

~~mark~~ that looks like

the outline of

an angel

or a ~~wilting~~

flower~~, or a~~

~~car crash~~

you're home

~~the entryway is~~
a mess of
of memories
and light
~~and fire~~

~~a cacophony~~
~~of constant mutterings~~
~~lies beneath the surface~~
~~and~~

~~the~~ walls
~~stretch thin~~
behind
pictures you
recognize ~~only~~
~~faintly~~

~~there's still~~
~~shit in the litter box,~~
and coffee grounds
in the french press

~~but~~ you smell

only the

~~dying~~

flowers

~~carve into your wood~~

~~house become~~
toy soldier
~~and~~ carry
everything but
your ~~soul~~

~~burn bright~~
~~like a witch~~
~~and pay~~
~~for the sins~~
~~you didn't mean~~
~~to get attached to~~

~~then collapse~~
~~a tired cluster~~
~~of resources~~
~~held together~~
~~by nothing~~
~~but dusty~~
memories

and ~~fool's~~

gold

~~leaving feels~~
~~like coming,~~
only ~~worse~~

~~the~~ home,
~~no longer~~
~~a home~~

hangs in
the air like
a ~~dying~~ star

~~insects die~~
~~into the ground~~
~~endlessly~~

~~the same way~~
~~they will the next~~
~~time~~

footprints and

scratchy sweaters

an imprint

on the wall that

looks like the

outline of an

angel or

a flower

you're home

a mess of

of memories

and light

24

walls behind

pictures you

recognize

and coffee

in the french

press

you smell

only the

flowers

toy soldier

carry everything

but your memories

and gold

only home

hangs in the air

like a star

Hourglass

It becomes much easier

To collapse in on oneself

Once the sand begins to

Overtake what else is left

The menial daily tasks

Like laundry or dishes

Are gone, arbitrary

And unavailable

And the day passes like

An old car,

Each exhalation

Filled with exhaust

The constant drone

Of hunger long gone,

Replaced with a

Blank placard

The sand only
Continues to drift in,
Housed nowhere
But here

Each step forward
Flings particles into
The air, and coats
My feet

With dusty layer
Over dusty layer
Soon I will have
No more hiding places

Once a thing is
Everywhere, the instances
Without become
Noteworthy in its absence

Lost memories appear
Sometimes, like allusions
To works known to
A younger version

Of myself:
A scar, just under
My shoulder arcing
Across my back

Like a bolt of
Lightning. "I must
Have been fast,
A runner" I say

It would be nice to
Trace the scar
But the sand has
Coated my hands

And I dislike being
Touched; The

Beauty mark on

My forearm

Used to remind me

Of an actor, but

It is hardly

Discernable now

And the actor

Is either long dead

Or retired; My eyes

Bloodshot and apathetic

Appear guilty

When I happen

Across the half-buried

Mirror, and lost.

The days pass into
Months, which pass
Into years

Rest was never
Meant to be
Permanent

But these things
Happen, you tell
Yourself

"This isn't so
Bad," you say
Softly

As though afraid
Of stirring up
Old emotions

The sand has
Caught up with

The rest of you

Your feet
Trapped beneath
Constant weight

Your eyes
Hardly more than
Accessories

And your thoughts
And arbitrations
meaningless

But these things
Never mattered
To you anyway

What you had
Was enough
It had to be

As the sand buries

you, abandonment

becomes easier

You realize what

Was important,

Who you were

And why you

Hurt so

Often

But even those things

Are so small and

Insignificant

The sand was

Hardly an issue

Until it was

As you continue

To pass, the pain

Becomes yearning

So much left
Unaccomplished,
So much undone

You had so much
Potential, so
Long ago

But the world was
Given to you
In portions

You could only see
So much before
Leaving

Soon, only a
Single thought
Remains

The sand already
Beginning to
Fall into your lungs

And each labored
Breath a dust
Cloud

"If only I knew,"
You splutter
To no one

Even as you
Perish, it weighs
On you:

You were always
Made of time

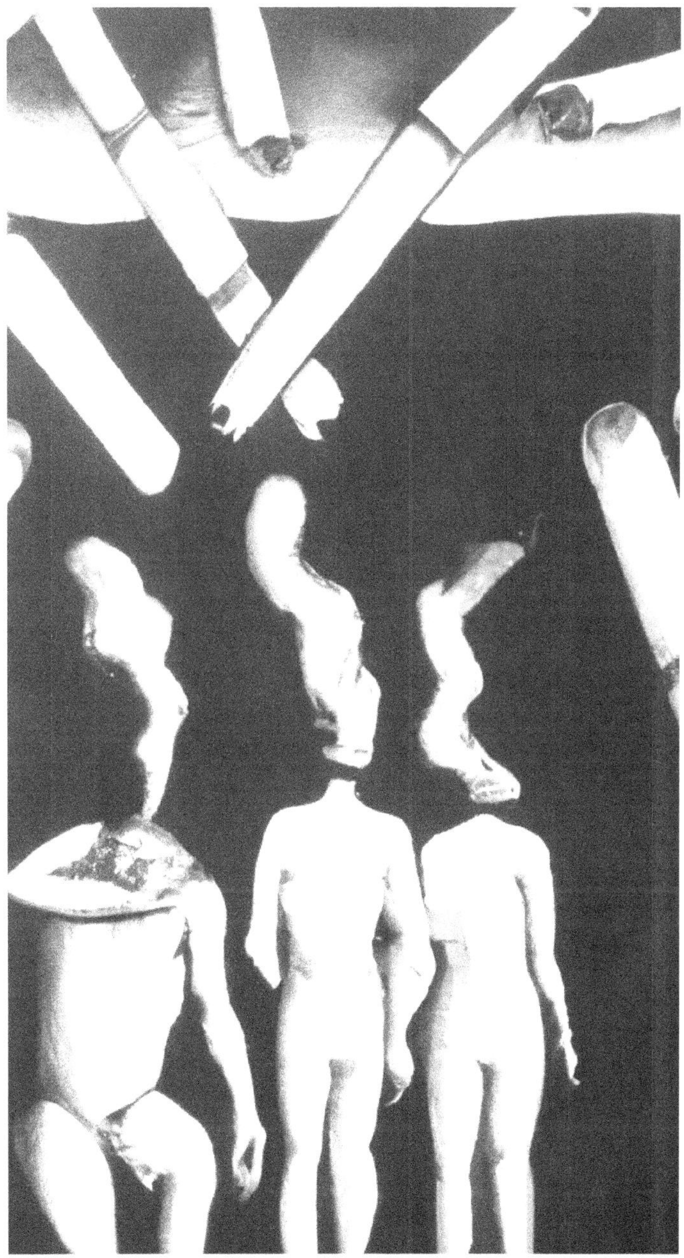